Investigating
CONTINENTS
AFRICA
A 4D Book

by Christine Juarez

PEBBLE
a capstone imprint

Download the Capstone app!

- Ask an adult to download the Capstone 4D app.
- Scan the cover and stars inside the book for additional content.

When you scan a spread, you'll find
fun extra stuff to go with this book!
You can also find these things
on the web at www.capstone4D.com
using the password: africa.27940

First Facts are published by Pebble,
1710 Roe Crest Drive, North Mankato, Minnesota 56003
www.mycapstone.com

Library of Congress Cataloging-in-Publication Data
Library of Congress Cataloging-in-Publication Data is on file with the Library of Congress.
ISBN 978-1-5435-2794-0 (library binding)
ISBN 978-1-5435-2800-8 (paperback)
ISBN 978-1-5435-2806-0 (ebook pdf)

Editorial Credits
Cynthia Della-Rovere and Clare Webber, designers; Svetlana Zhurkin, media researcher;
Kathy McColley, production specialist

Photo Credits
Capstone Global Library Ltd, 5, 9; Shutterstock: aaabbbccc, 17, Al Pidgen, 11, Alta Oosthuizen, 13, Anton_
Ivanov, 10, BlueOrange Studio, 15 (back), cornfield, 19, Dan Breckwoldt, 7, Elzbieta Sekowska, cover (top),
ixpert, cover (bottom right), back cover, 1, 3, Lukasz Janyst, 8, Mark Coran, cover (bottom left), Oksana
Byelikova, 15 (inset), Prin Adulyatham, cover (middle), Sarine Arslanian, 21, tatyana enotova (pattern),
cover (left) and throughout

Table of Contents

About Africa

Africa is one of the largest **continents**. Only Asia is bigger than Africa. One half of Africa is north of the **equator**. The other half is south of the equator.

Africa is almost surrounded by water. The Atlantic Ocean is to the west. To the east is the Indian Ocean. The Mediterranean Sea is to the north. The Southern Ocean is south of Africa.

PACIFIC OCEAN

continent—one of Earth's seven large land masses

equator—an imaginary line around the middle of Earth

ARCTIC OCEAN

CONTINENTS OF THE WORLD

NORTH AMERICA

EUROPE

ASIA

ATLANTIC OCEAN

MEDITERRANEAN SEA

AFRICA

EQUATOR

INDIAN OCEAN

SOUTH AMERICA

AUSTRALIA

SOUTHERN OCEAN

ANTARCTICA

Famous Places

The **Pyramids** of Giza are one famous place in Africa. The pyramids are in the country of Egypt. They were built 4,500 years ago.

The amazing Victoria Falls are on the Zambezi River. This famous waterfall is 5,604 feet (1,708 meters) wide.

pyramid—a solid building with sloping sides that come together at the top; the pyramids in Egypt were built as places to bury rulers, called pharaohs

Pyramids of Giza in Egypt

Geography

Different **landforms** are found in Africa. Huge deserts stretch across Africa's northern and southern parts. The Sahara Desert covers almost all of North Africa. The Namib Desert and the Kalahari Desert are in the south. Grassy plains cover parts of Africa. Huge rain forests grow along the equator.

Fact: The highest point in Africa is Mount Kilimanjaro. Its peak is 19,340 feet (5,895 m) high.

landform—a feature of an area, including mountains, hills, deserts, and canyons

LANDFORMS OF AFRICA

Sahara Desert

AFRICA

EQUATOR

N
W E
S

Mount Kilimanjaro

Namib Desert

Kalahari Desert

The Nile is the longest river in the world. It starts in the middle of Africa and flows to the Mediterranean Sea. Africa has other major rivers. They are the Congo, Niger, and Zambezi Rivers.

Fact: The Nile River is 4,132 miles (6,650 kilometers) long.

Zambezi River

Nile River

Weather

The weather in Africa is hot most of the time. The weather along the equator is hot and wet all year round. It rains almost every day in the rain forests. In the grasslands, there is a dry season and a rainy season. But in the deserts, it is dry year-round. It is very hot during the day and cold at night.

Dark storm clouds bring rain to grasslands in southern Africa.

Animals

Africa is full of wildlife. On the grasslands, elephants, giraffes, and lions are found. Herds of zebras and other animals live there too. In rain forests are gorillas and all kind of birds. Some animals on the island of Madagascar cannot be found anywhere else in the world. Lemurs are one example.

African elephants

ring-tailed lemurs

Plants

Many unusual plants grow in Africa. Plants grow well in the warm, wet rain forests. Mahogany and ebony trees grow tall there. The wide baobab trees grow on grasslands. Palm trees are in deserts. Orchids and African violets are just a few of the different kinds of flowers in Africa.

baobab trees

People

People live in 56 different countries in Africa. More than 1,500 native languages are spoken. People in Africa might also speak English, French, or Arabic.

Many Africans live in a city. Cairo in Egypt has the largest **population**. In the countryside, people live in small villages. The people there farm or look after herds of animals.

Fact: Africa's population is about 1.2 billion people.

population—the number of people who live in an area

Cairo, Egypt

Natural Resources and Products

Africa has many **natural resources**. Diamonds and gold are mined from the ground in South Africa. Oil is found in North and West Africa.

Africa's resources also include crops. Farmers grow them to eat, sell, or send to other countries. Coffee, tea, and bananas are common crops.

natural resource—a material from nature that is useful to people

A man sells bananas at a market in the country of Uganda.

Glossary

continent (KAHN-tuh-nuhnt)—one of Earth's seven large land masses

equator (i-KWAY-tuhr)—an imaginary line around the middle of Earth; it divides the northern and southern halves

landform (LAND-form)—a feature of an area, including mountains, hills, deserts, and canyons

natural resource (NACH-ur-uhl REE-sorss)—a material from nature that is useful to people

population (pop-yuh-LAY-shuhn)—the number of people who live in an area

pyramid (PIHR-uh-mid)—a solid building with sloping sides that come together at the top; the pyramids in Egypt were built as places to bury rulers, called pharaohs

Read More

Aspen-Baxter, Linda. *Africa*. Exploring Our Seven Continents. New York: AV2 by Weigl, 2018.

Rockett, Paul. *Mapping Africa*. Mapping the Continents. St. Catharines, Ont.: Crabtree Publishing Company, 2017.

Internet Sites

Use FactHound to find Internet sites related to this book.

Visit *www.facthound.com*

Just type in 9781543527940 and go.

Super-cool stuff!

Check out projects, games and lots more at
www.capstonekids.com

⭐ Critical Thinking Questions

1. What crops do farmers grow in Africa?
2. Describe some of the plants and trees that grow in Africa.
3. The text on page 14 describes some of Africa's animals. Which of these animals would you most like to see? Why?

Index